JENNY ERICKSON

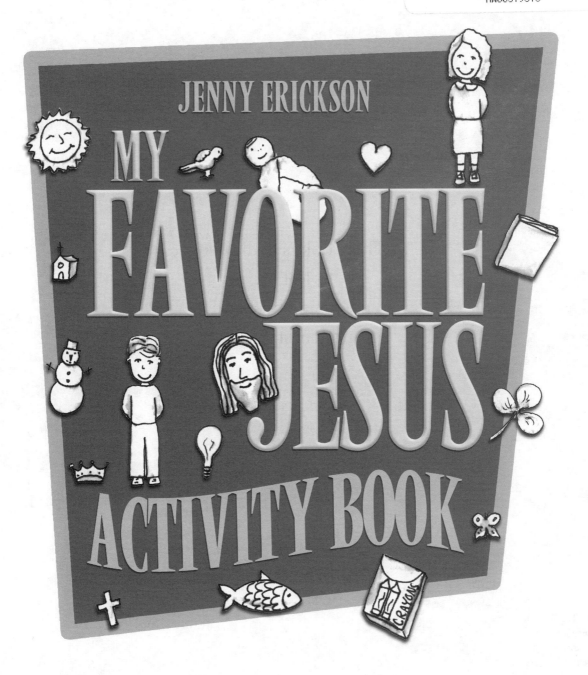

MY FAVORITE JESUS

ACTIVITY BOOK

TWENTY-THIRD PUBLICATIONS

Bayard

185 WILLOW STREET • PO BOX 180 • MYSTIC, CT 06355
TEL: 1-800-321-0411 • FAX: 1-800-572-0788
E-MAIL: ttpubs@aol.com • www.twentythirdpublications.com

Dedication

This book is dedicated
to Robert,
my loving husband
and truest friend

Twenty-Third Publications
A Division of Bayard
185 Willow Street
P.O. Box 180
Mystic, CT 06355
(860) 536-2611
(800) 321-0411
www.twentythirdpublications.com

ISBN:1-58595-200-1
Printed in the U.S.A.

Contents

Lent

April

May

End of the School Year

Introduction

Educators face an enormous challenge today. The mighty world of computer, Nintendo, internet, and cable have accustomed our youngsters to fast-moving animation and entertainment.

Parents and schoolteachers juggle and struggle, searching for ways to make the material interesting enough, not only to help children remember but to keep them happily coming back for more.

Religious educators, of course, experience the same thing. Only they have a triple challenge: their kids not only need to know the lessons; they need to be motivated to make the right moral choices. And, above all, children need to experience God's love and friendship, as the psalmist says, "O God, you are my God, I seek you, my soul thirsts for you" (Ps 63:1).

As a parent or teacher of religious education, you are not alone in the task of faith formation. God is with you. With personal moments spent in prayer, Scripture readings, or some moments of personal meditation, you will be able to nourish your own faith, first of all. Having done that, you can share the wonders of our faith with your children.

My Favorite Jesus Activity Book is designed to make faith formation an enjoyable time of learning for your children. Activities include word searches, crossword puzzles, pictograms, prayers, scriptural trivia, calendar of the saints, crafts, gift ideas, and more. As the book follows a monthly format, kids become familiar with the seasons and the liturgical year. And best of all, they will have fun doing it!

The pages are reproducible. Catechists and religion teachers have permission to make copies for the children in their religion classes. Each month you will find some suggestions on how to use the material. You can use the prayers with your children, or copy them for the youngsters to hang in their rooms.

May God bless you and your children. Take inspiration from the words of the prophet Daniel: "Those who are wise shall shine like the brightness of the sky, and those who lead many to righteousness, like the stars forever and ever" (Dan 12:3).

Month of September

O Lord,

You gave me a mind to think and learn.

You gave me a heart to love and care.

You gave me the freedom to choose between good and bad.

Bless me during this school year.

Help me always use your gifts in ways

that will please you.

And most of all, Lord,

Remind me each day to tell you

how much I love you.

Amen.

Note to Parents and Teachers

September is a month of beginnings. The activities for this month focus on the start of the new school year. They aim to help your children keep in touch with God, and to look ahead to what the year might bring. Help them start their journal and make their special booklet. Talk about these activities, as well as the others that follow. Find out what they learn from them. Golden Rule and Along the Way (about God's gifts) can be used any time during the year.

Children's Calendar of the Saints

SEPTEMBER

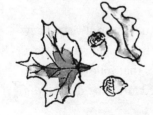

1	2	3	4	5	6	7
		St. Gregory the Great				
8	9	10	11	12	13	14
Birth of Mary	St. Peter Claver				St. John Chrysostom	Triumph of the Holy Cross
15	16	17	18	19	20	21
Our Lady of Sorrows	Saints Cornelius and Cyprian	St. Robert Bellarmine		St. Januarius	St. Andrew Kim Taegon, St. Paul Ch'ong Hasang and Companions	St. Matthew, Apostle
22	23	24	25	26	27	28
				Saints Cosmas and Damian	St. Vincent de Paul	St. Wenceslaus, St. Lawrence Ruiz and Companions
29	30					
Saints Michael, Gabriel & Raphael, Archangels	St. Jerome					

Window to My Heart
My Personal Journal

Every year around this time, you may see some of your old classmates again. You can tell them about some wonderful things you did during the summer. Then the year goes by. Day by day. Month by month. By springtime, you will have many memories to think about. Now you can begin a book of all your favorite memories—a book that you can write yourself! Take some time during the week to write in your journal. Here are some things you can write about in these pages:

- Sad or happy feelings you have had
- Things that have upset or scared you
- Places you went, people you met
- Favorite holidays, hobbies, sports, or memories
- Things you want to tell Jesus
- Stories in the Bible you heard about
- Important lessons you learned in religion class
- Prayers

Do you know how people get to know you? Your words tell a big part of what you are thinking and feeling. When you look through a window of a house, you can see what is happening inside. That is the same with your words in your journal. When you (or anyone else you share this with) read the words you write, you and they can understand better what is going on in your mind and heart. Your journal is a window to your heart.

Activity
Materials: Markers, crayons, scissors, glue, a new wide-lined notebook
Instructions: Decorate and cut out the window on the following page. Glue it to the front cover of a wide-lined notebook. On the first page inside the notebook, glue the poem, "Window to My Heart." Then make a special page about yourself and your name.

Whenever you have time to write in your journal, either during the time your teacher allows or before you go to bed, write about the things that are important to you. This will be a special keepsake for you always.

Decorate and cut out this window. Glue it to the front of your journal.

Window to my Heart

Here is my Journal. When I read it I see
that everything here
is all about me!

I read about secrets I wrote down before.
I said what I liked, where I went,
and much more.

I wrote about moments when I was feeling bad,
but then there were fun times
that made me so glad!

I'm happy that I kept a memory of things
that I learned about God
and the love that God brings.

Sometimes I even wrote the words I would say
to my best friend, Jesus,
who is with me each day.

I know I am special; I am God's work of art,
and these things that I wrote are like
a window to my heart.

Month of September

"I Am Very Special" Coloring Booklet

Directions: To make this into a booklet, fold each sheet in half horizontally so that "My name" is on the outside corner. On the second sheet, "God loves Me!" will be on the front. Insert and staple the folded side edge. Then fold it again vertically.

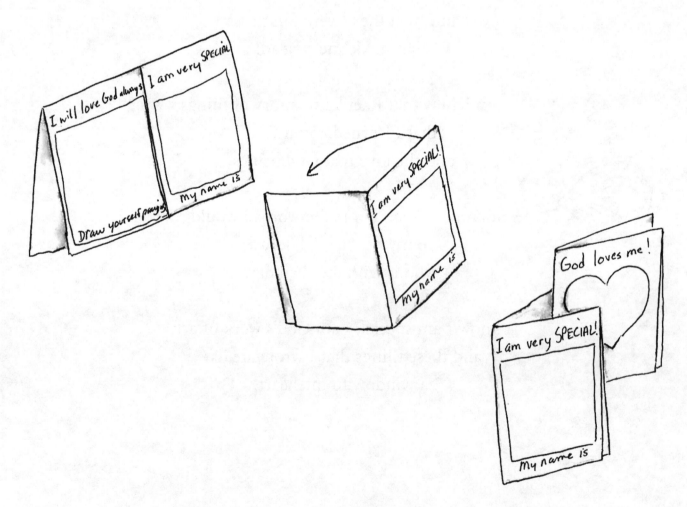

My name is _____

Draw a picture of yourself.

I am very SPECIAL!

Draw yourself praying.

I will love God always.

God watches over me…

Draw yourself sleeping.

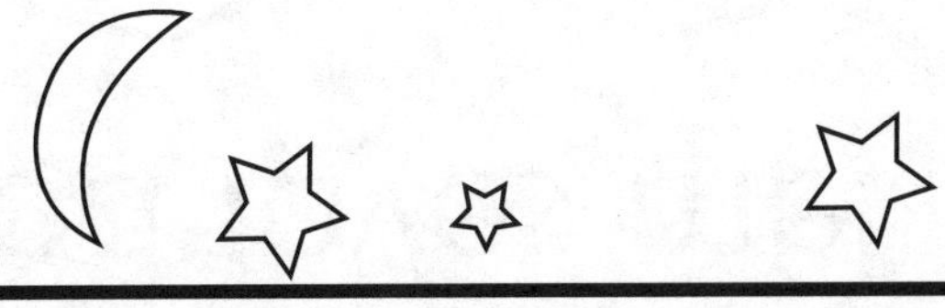

even when I am sleeping.

God gave me special people who love me.

Draw someone you love.

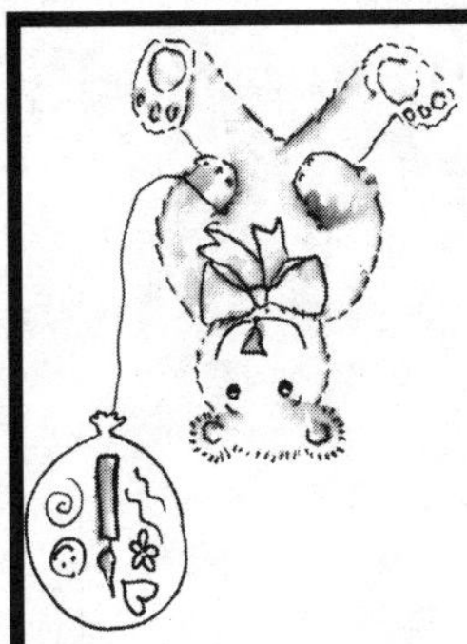

Color and decorate the heart.

God loves me!

Draw some things
God has given you.

God gives me
many things

God made me!

Draw yourself
when you were a baby.

God even knows
what I am thinking.

Draw something
you are thinking about

The Golden Rule Cryptoquip

Now you start a new school year! You are going to learn a lot of things. You will have lots of fun, too. You will play with your school friends. Some kids you know might not be your friends. You may even not like some of them. But Jesus told us that we must try hard to be kind to others. Fill in the letters, following the code, to see what Jesus said about the Golden Rule. The first word is done for you.

1=O	8=A	15=E	22=K
2=H	9=V	16=X	23=R
3=B	10=T	17=G	24=W
4=L	11=J	18=D	25=U
5=Q	12=C	19=P	26=Z
6=M	13=S	20=I	
7=F	14=N	21=Y	

$$\underset{10}{T}\ \underset{23}{R}\ \underset{15}{E}\ \underset{8}{A}\ \underset{10}{T}\qquad \underset{1}{\_}\ \underset{10}{\_}\ \underset{2}{\_}\ \underset{15}{\_}\ \underset{23}{\_}\ \underset{13}{\_}$$

$$\underset{8}{\_}\ \underset{13}{\_}\qquad \underset{21}{\_}\ \underset{1}{\_}\ \underset{25}{\_}\qquad \underset{24}{\_}\ \underset{1}{\_}\ \underset{25}{\_}\ \underset{4}{\_}\ \underset{18}{\_}$$

$$\underset{4}{\_}\ \underset{20}{\_}\ \underset{22}{\_}\ \underset{15}{\_}\qquad \underset{10}{\_}\ \underset{2}{\_}\ \underset{15}{\_}\ \underset{6}{\_}\qquad \underset{10}{\_}\ \underset{1}{\_}$$

$$\underset{10}{\_}\ \underset{23}{\_}\ \underset{15}{\_}\ \underset{8}{\_}\ \underset{10}{\_}\qquad \underset{21}{\_}\ \underset{1}{\_}\ \underset{25}{\_}\qquad \textbf{(Mt 7:12)}$$

11

Month of September

Along the Way Maze

What if someone thought of you every day, all day long, and gave you gifts continuously? Did you know that there is someone who does that? God thinks of you all the time. And God's gifts are all around you, even when you don't realize it. Below, help Jill find her way to school. Then read the poem that she wrote for religion class.

Thank You, Lord

I ride my bike to school each day. I look at things along the way.
I think that I am glad to see all the wonders God gives to me!
God made for me the sun and sky, and lets me watch the birds that fly.
I like to study the ants and bees, and pick a leaf as I pass the trees.
The flowers give off a scent so sweet, and I love the green grass beneath my feet.
I know it's important to stop and pray...and thank God for his gifts each day!

Month of September

Pack Your Backpack! Match-Up

Circle the things you need to pack in your backpack.

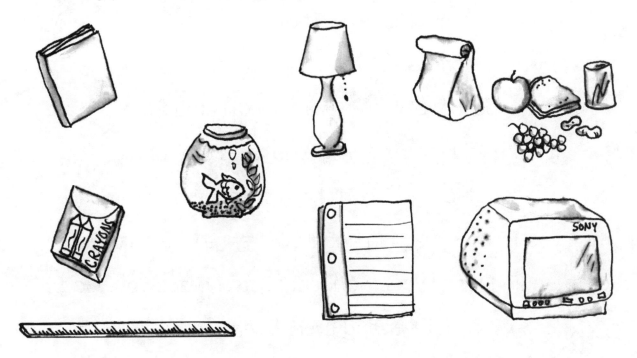

Now circle the things you need to do to have a good year at school.

Play fair   Pray to God   Bully others   Study

Behave   Talk back   Respect teachers   Listen

Decide which of these you want to try very hard to do this year.
These can be your resolutions (promises) for the new school year.

Month of October

Heavenly Father,

I praise you for all of creation,

for the beauty of nature that I see all around me.

I praise you for the family who takes care of me

and for the friends I can share with.

I praise you for the guardian angel you sent to watch over me.

For these and for all your wonderful gifts, I praise you, God.

forever and ever! Amen.

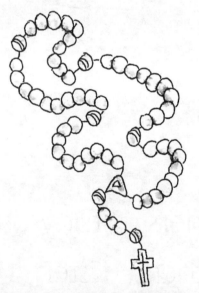

Note to Parents and Teachers

In this month of angels, of harvest time, and of the rosary, you can help your youngsters enjoy the splendor of God's creation. One activity focuses on the guardian angel as friend and protector. Another takes the image of the tree with its changing leaves, and asks the children to make a family tree poster. The crossword puzzle and "Follow the Leader!" offer ways of talking about how we follow Jesus. These and the Fun with Numbers Bible Match may be used throughout the year. It offers a good opportunity for learning how to look for quotes in the Bible.

Children's Calendar of the Saints

OCTOBER

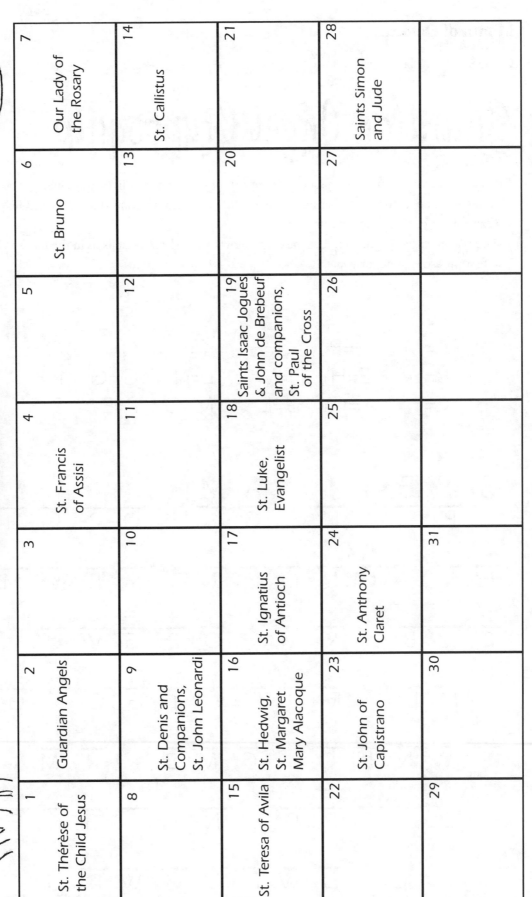

1 St. Thérèse of the Child Jesus	**2** Guardian Angels	**3**	**4** St. Francis of Assisi	**5**	**6** St. Bruno	**7** Our Lady of the Rosary
8	**9** St. Denis and Companions, St. John Leonardi	**10**	**11**	**12**	**13**	**14** St. Callistus
15 St. Teresa of Avila	**16** St. Hedwig, St. Margaret Mary Alacoque	**17** St. Ignatius of Antioch	**18** St. Luke, Evangelist	**19** Saints Isaac Jogues & John de Brebeuf and companions, St. Paul of the Cross	**20**	**21**
22	**23** St. John of Capistrano	**24** St. Anthony Claret	**25**	**26**	**27**	**28** Saints Simon and Jude
29	**30**	**31**				

Month of October

October 2, Guardian Angels

Guardian Angel Cryptoquip

Today the Church celebrates someone very important in each of our lives: our Guardian Angel. God has given each of us a special angel to watch over us during our life on earth. Our angel loves us and helps us grow close to God. We can call on our angel to help us anytime.

   Here is a message to figure out. Use the code below to see what God tells us in the Bible about our Guardian Angel. The first phrase is done for you.

A=M	D=P	G=A	K=V	N=I	Q=S	U=D
B=U	E=H	I=W	L=N	O=G	R=T	V=F
C=Y	F=C	J=L	M=O	P=E	S=B	W=R

S E E   I   A M   __ __ __ __ __ __ __
Q P P   N   G A   Q P L U N L O

__ __   __ __ __ __ __   __ __ __ __ __ __
G L   G L O P J   S P V M W P

__ __ __   __ __   __ __ __ __ __   __ __ __
C M B   R M   O B G W U   C M B

__ __   __ __ __   __ __ __   __ __ __
M L   R E P   I G C   G L U

__ __ __ __ __   __ __ __   __ __   __ __ __
S W N L O   C M B   R M   R E P

__ __ __ __ __   __   __ __ __ __
D J G F P   N   E G K P

__ __ __ __ __ __ __ __
D W P D G W P U

(Ex 23:20)

16

Family Tree Craft

In October, we see the leaves on the trees have turned different beautiful colors. Many have even fallen to the ground. See how nature changes!

Your family is like a strong tree, growing and changing. The leaves are like the members of your family: you, your grandparents, your aunts and uncles, your parents, your brothers and sisters. Your family is so special to God. Your family is so special to you!

Here is a poster you can make that tells about you and your family.

Materials: Poster paper, chalk, construction paper of different colors, glue, markers

1. On a dark sheet of paper, trace your foot with just your sock on. (Chalk shows up better on dark paper than does pencil.) Cut out and glue this to the poster paper. This will be the "trunk" of the tree.

2. Then, trace your hand, fingers outstretched on top of brown paper. Cut out and glue this to the top of the trunk. The fingers will be the branches of your tree.

3. Now, with the help of an adult, cut leaves out of different colored sheets of construction paper. You can use the leaf pattern below or make your own. On each leaf, put the name of one of your family members. Glue the leaves to the branches.

4. Finally, at the bottom (or top) of the poster, write with markers, "(Your name)'s Family Tree."

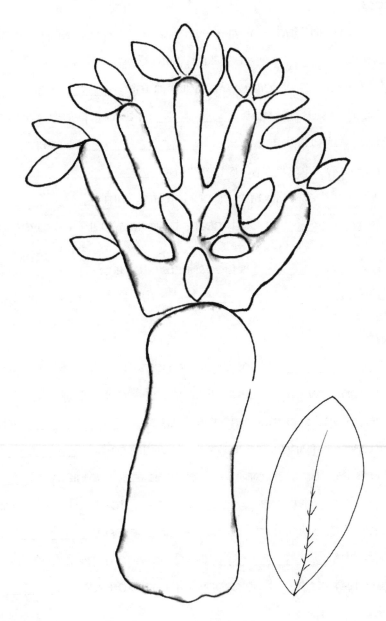

Month of October

Growing in God Fill-In

Complete the sentences below using a word from this list. (Use each word only once.)
Then use the answers to complete the crossword on the next page.

Peace   Respect   Bible   Heaven   Church   Christ   Happy   Sacraments   Thankful

Honest   Sorry   Forgive   Pray   Honor   Trust   Defend   Truth   Courage   Love

Across

1. We worship God together every Sunday. A special place of worship is called a _____.

2. When we ____, we are talking with God.

7. We celebrate the gift of God's life in the _____.

10. God asks us to show _____ to our parents and teachers.

12. Jesus tells us that we should _____ our neighbor as ourselves.

13. The opposite of lying is to tell the _____.

15. When I thank God for all of His gifts, I am _____.

16. _____ in God means believing that God loves me and will help me when things are hard.

17. The _____ is God's "letter" to us.

18. Jesus asks us to _____ others when they hurt us.

Down

1. _____ means "the anointed one."

3. St. Francis wrote a beautiful prayer called the _____ prayer.

4. The second commandment tells us to _____ God's name.

5. Instead of giving in to jealousy, I will try to be _____ that other kids have done well.

6. If kids pick on someone weaker than them, I will try to _____ that person.

8. Holy Spirit, give me _____ to stand up for what is right.

9. When I do something wrong, I tell God how _____ I am.

11. I will be _____ in school and at play. Cheaters never win in the end.

14. God wants me to be happy with him forever in _____.

Month of October

Growing in God Crossword

Fill in the crossword with the answers from page 18.
You will know your answers are right if they fit into the crossword.

Month of October

Follow the Leader Pictogram

Have you ever played "Follow the leader?" It's a very fun game. The person in front gets to be the leader and you have to do everything he or she does. If he jumps, you jump. If she hops, you hop.

During your life right now and even when you grow up, you will have to make many choices. You need someone to help you and guide you. You need a leader to follow. Who is the best leader? Figure out the puzzle to find out! Look at the picture below each line. What letter does that picture start with? Write it on the line.

20

Fun with Numbers Bible Match

See how many Scripture numbers you know. Choose the correct number from the list to complete each sentence below. Use each number only one time. If you are not sure of the answer, read the Bible story by yourself or with someone in your family who can help you.

one   two   three   four   five   six
seven   eight   nine   ten   eleven   twelve

A. Jesus told the waiters at the wedding feast of Cana to fill _____ stone jars with water. Then Jesus changed the water into wine. (John 2:1–12)

B. Peter denied Jesus _____ times. (Luke 22:54–62)

C. Jesus' friend Lazarus was in the tomb for _____ days. Jesus raised him from the dead. (John 11:32–44)

D. When Jesus was _____ years old, Mary and Joseph took him to the temple in Jerusalem. (Luke 2:41–50)

E. Jesus fed a whole crowd of people with just _____ loaves of bread and _____ fish. (Mark 6:34–44)

F. Jesus told the story of a man with one hundred sheep. _____ of the sheep got lost. (Matthew 18:12–14)

G. Peter asked Jesus how many times we should forgive someone. Jesus said you should forgive seventy times _____ times. (Matthew 18:21–22)

H. Jesus tells the story about _____ bridesmaids. Some were foolish and some were wise. (Matthew 25:1–13)

I. After Jesus' death, _____ of the apostles gathered together in hiding. (Mark 16:14)

J. In the "Sermon on the Mount," Jesus taught us the _____ beatitudes. (Matthew 5:1–12)

K. Jesus cured some lepers. One came back to thank him; the other _____ did not. (Luke 17:12–19)

Loving God,

During this month we pray

for all the people who have died.

We especially pray for members of our family.

Please comfort those who are sad.

We also celebrate the people

who lived holy lives.

We ask them to pray for us.

Dear God, watch over us all.

Help us remember that you are right beside us,

loving us every step of the way.

Amen.

Note to Parents and Teachers

All Saints Day offers an opportunity to talk about Christian witnesses who are good role models for your children. Have an All Saints Day party, and let the kids wear their "Let Your Light Shine" buttons. The activities about Jesus calming the storm help them learn about Jesus' care for us. Celebrate Christ the King by helping your youngsters connect the dots and make paper crowns. If you haven't already done the Family Tree activity from October, you might like to use that as a Thanksgiving Day activity.

Children's Calendar of the Saints

NOVEMBER

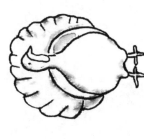

1	2	3	4	5	6	7
All Saints Day	All Souls Day	St. Martin de Porres	St. Charles Borromeo			
8	**9** Dedication of St. John Lateran Basilica	**10** St. Leo the Great	**11** St. Martin of Tours	**12** St. Josaphat	**13** St. Frances Xavier Cabrini	**14**
15 St. Albert the Great	**16** St. Margaret of Scotland, St. Gertrude the Great	**17** St. Elizabeth of Hungary	**18** Dedication of the Basilicas of Peter & Paul, St. Rose Philippine Duchesne	**19**	**20**	**21** Presentation of Mary
22 St. Cecilia	**23** St. Clement I, St.Columban, Blessed Miguel Augustin Pro	**24** St. Andrew Dung-Lac and Companions	**25**	**26**	**27**	**28**
29	**30** St. Andrew, Apostle	**31**				

November 1, All Saints Day

Let Your Light Shine! Craft

On All Saints Day we think about all the great saints who have gone before us. But we also take a look at the saints living among us! Make a button to remind yourself (and others) that you, too, want to be like Jesus.

Materials: Markers, glitter, self-adhesive velcro or safety pins, scissors

Directions: Cut out the buttons below and decorate them with markers, glitter, etc. Place your name under the word Saint. Then Velcro (or pin) one of them to your shirt.

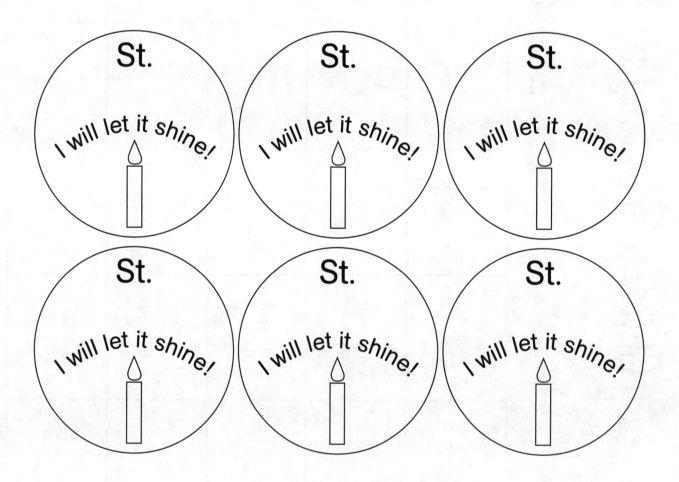

Jesus Calms the Storm Rebus

Sometimes things happen that we aren't used to. We go to a new school, have a new classmate or teacher in school. Or our school schedule changes. Some changes can be fun. Some can make us nervous. No matter what happens, Jesus teaches us not to worry because he is always with us.

One day Jesus' disciples were very frightened. They were out in the middle of the sea. When a bad storm arose, they thought the boat would capsize and they would drown. Jesus was in the boat but he was sleeping. The disciples woke him up.

Jesus spoke to the wind and the sea. Everything grew calm. Then the disciples realized Jesus had power even over the scariest things.

Jesus, I trust in you!

Can you figure out the rebus?

They said:

 S +   - W    - B   L +  - SW

_____ _____ _____

Jesus asked them:

"Y"    - C   U   FR +  - L   N+D

_____ _____ _____ _____

Jesus Is Your Friend Match-up

Jesus and his friends went for a boat ride. Jesus got tired and fell asleep. Suddenly, a bad storm came. The wind tossed the boat. Waves splashed Jesus' friends. They were scared. They said, "Jesus, wake up! Help us!" Jesus woke up. He told the wind, "Be quiet." And the wind became quiet. He told the sea, "Be calm." And the sea became calm. The storm went away. Jesus saved his friends. His friends knew Jesus was God.
Remember this story. Jesus is your friend. He will always help you!

Now, look at each picture in the left column. Find and circle the matching picture on the right.

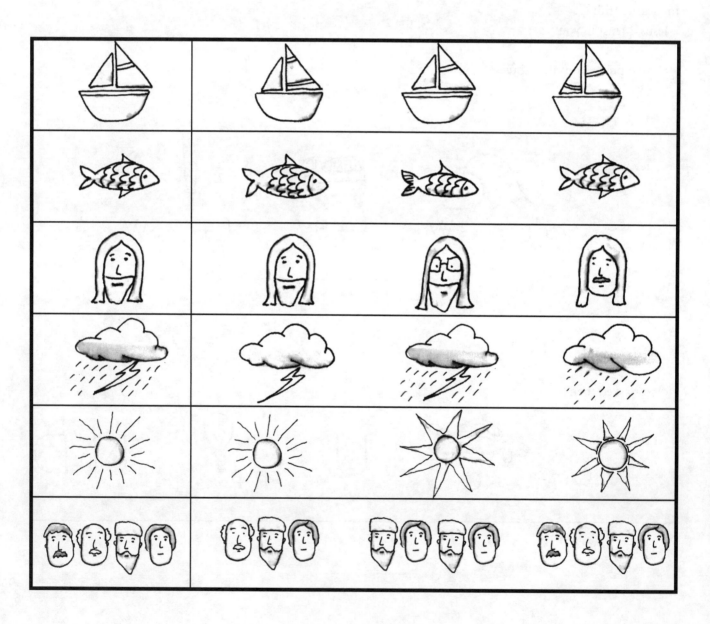

Month of November

Feast of Christ the King

Jesus Is our King! Connect the Dots

Jesus is our king. He is the greatest King! We want Jesus to be king of our hearts and our lives. Connect the dots, then color and decorate the picture. See what you can make for Jesus.

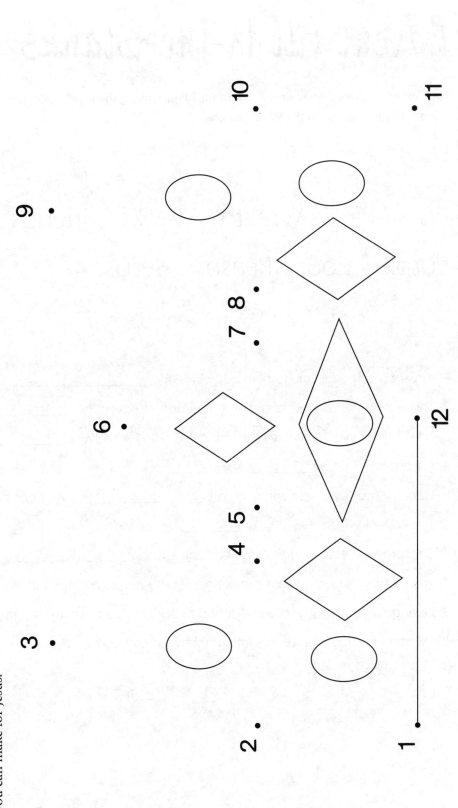

Advent Fill-In-The-Blanks

How many answers do you know? Fill in the blanks, using the words below.
Then find these words in the Word Search.

Pray   Pink   Wreath   Weeks   Friends   Christmas

Purple   Four   Reason   Jesus

1. Advent is a special time to help us prepare for_____.

2. The color the Church uses during the season of Advent is _____.

3. The circle of evergreen with candles in it is called an Advent _____.

4. Advent lasts for four _____.

5. During Advent we set aside time to _____ with our family.

6. The Advent wreath has _____ candles.

7. One prayer we say during Advent is "Come, Lord _____, come!"

8. Three of the Advent wreath candles are usually purple and the other one is _____.

9. During Advent, we try to be extra kind to our sisters and brothers and _____.

10. When Christmas comes, it is important to remember that Jesus is the _____

for the season!

Advent Word Search

B	U	A	D	G	W	F	J
O	C	P	I	N	K	R	O
L	H	V	M	U	S	I	T
W	R	E	A	T	H	E	M
A	I	H	W	M	O	N	E
D	S	O	P	A	R	D	F
E	T	K	R	B	L	S	G
I	M	Z	A	S	E	L	K
P	A	N	Y	V	M	I	R
U	S	E	F	R	O	Z	E
R	H	I	G	C	P	N	A
P	R	U	J	E	S	U	S
L	A	C	Z	D	I	K	O
E	M	F	O	U	R	B	N
S	O	D	B	N	V	U	C
T	W	E	E	K	S	F	I

Jesus,

you are the Son of God.

You came to us as a tiny baby.

You came to earth as our brother,

to bless the world with your presence.

Help us understand

the real meaning of Christmas.

Then on Christmas Day

we will kneel near your crib

with the angels, the shepherds, and the kings.

We will sing, Glory to God!

Amen.

Note to Parents and Teachers

More than anyone, children enter into the mystery of Christmas with a sense of wonder. Use these activities to help your youngsters focus on the true meaning and message of the Christmas season.

Children's Calendar of the Saints

DECEMBER

1	2	3 St. Francis Xavier	4 St. John Damascene	5	6 St. Nicholas	7 St. Ambrose
8 Immaculate Conception of the Blessed Virgin Mary	9	10	11 St. Damasus I	12 Our Lady of Guadalupe, St. Jane Frances de Chantel	13 St. Lucy	14 St. John of the Cross
15	16	17	18	19	20	21 St. Peter Canisius
22	23 St. John of Kanty	24 Christmas Eve	25 Christmas Day Nativity of the Lord	26 St. Stephen	27 St. John, Apostle	28 Holy Innocents
29 St. Thomas Becket	30	31 St. Sylvester I				

Christmas Match

Think about the story of Jesus' birth. Look at all the pictures. Connect each of the pictures on the right with the picture on the left that matches it best. Then color the pictures and use them to tell the Christmas story.

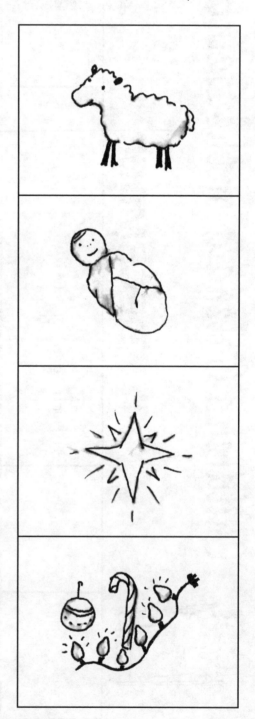

Christmas Word Search

Find these 40 hidden words below. The words go up, down, across, diagonally, even backwards. What does each one have to do with Christmas?

ADESTE FIDELIS	FRANKINCENSE	JOY	NOEL	SHEEP
ADORE	GIFTS	LORD	PEACE	SHEPHERDS
ANGELS	GOLD	LOVE	PRAISE	SILENT NIGHT
BABY JESUS	GRACE	MANGER	PROMISE	SON OF GOD
BETHLEHEM	HAY	MARY	PURE	STAR
CHRISTMAS	HOPE	MESSIAH	REDEEMER	THREE KINGS
COW	INN	MOTHER OF GOD	SALVATION	TOWN
DONKEY	JOSEPH	MYRRH	SAVIOR	WORSHIP

```
A N G E L S P U R E R O D A T
D Z R C T H R E E K I N G S H
E R A O S E H A Y N W O T T G
S B C W S P M R E G N A M F I
T A E M E H P Y O J R O R I N
E B Y S A E E L R E J A E G T
F Y O P Y R D E V R N L F L N
I J B R E D Y O P K H H O P E
D E E O K S L F I E C A E P L
E S T M N S O N O F G O D R I
L U H I O M C H R I S T M A S
I S L S D E H A I S S E M I A
S D E E N W O R S H I P E S V
N R H S A L V A T I O N B E I
N O E B T R E D E E M E R K O
I L M O T H E R O F G O D N R
```

Christmas Scramble

Unscramble the words below to find out what we can say with the angels, the shepherds, the three wise men, and everyone who went to see baby Jesus that first Christmas. Write the words in the spaces below. Then color the picture.

HO MOEC TLE SU DRAEO MHI!

__ ____ ___ __ ____ __

Landon's Gift

A Christmas Skit to Read Aloud or Act Out

Characters: Landon, Angel, Mom, Dad, Sister, Brother, Mary and Joseph, Baby Jesus

SCENE I

Landon's bedroom. A picture of a window with a black sky and a moon hangs on the wall behind the bed, indicating that it is night.

Landon What can I give Jesus for his birthday this year? Maybe he'd like a tent or a boat or fishing gear. Should I buy him a computer or a remote-control car? Or a telescope that's strong enough to find the farthest star? Would he like some electronic toys to keep him busy at play? I just wish I knew what to get for his birthday!

(Lights out.)

SCENE II

(Change picture on wall to window with sun outside and anything to indicate daytime. Landon wakes up, sits up with an angry face. Throws his feet over the side and speaks out loud.)

Landon (Loud and angry) I'm grouchy and I'm mad; my whole night was bad!!

(He gets up, stamps across stage left and mimics opening a door. Mom is at stage right and yells to him, as if she is in another room.)

Mom A friend is on the phone...

Landon (everything he says is said in a grumpy, huffy tone) Just tell him to leave me alone!

(Mom looks annoyed. Little sister comes up to him with her shoes untied.)

Sister Will you please tie my shoe?

Landon No. I don't want to. (Sister walks out with hurt look. Landon walks stage front, brother comes on stage.)

Brother You better take the garbage out. Remember that's your chore.

Landon I'll do it later. My feet are sore. (Brother rolls eyes.)

(Lights off stage. Night picture on wall again. Lights back on. Landon in front of TV. Father comes in.)

Father Turn the TV off and do your homework, Son.

Landon (aside) Oh why do grown-ups always ruin the fun?

(Landon gets up goes out to his bedroom. Mom, with a laundry basket, "opens" his door and peeks in.)

Mom Don't make me tell you again. You know what I said...

(Mom shuts the door and walks off. Landon wags his head, and uses a sassy, mimicking voice.)

Landon I know— "Landon, it's time to go to bed."

(Landon lies down and closes his eyes. Angel comes in, spreads her arms out over him and speaks to him while he sleeps.)

Angel Jesus doesn't want a pile of Tonka trucks or cars.

He doesn't need a telescope to show him all the stars.

It doesn't make him smile to see you standing there with toys.

He only wants you to bring others many joys.

Like kindness to your friends and patience with your sister, too,

And doing your chores even when you don't want to.

He likes to see that you obey your mom and dad always,

and do it without a sassy voice or a grumpy face.

(Pause) These are the gifts Jesus likes.

SCENE III

(Daytime. Landon sits on a chair or couch, reading. Mom walks through wearing a coat. She is on her way out to the store.)

Mom Landon, don't forget...

Landon (cheerfully) OK, Mom, I'll feed the cat. (Mom looks surprised and leaves stage. Little sister comes in, looking sad.)

Sister (To Landon) I spilled my paint. Can you help me right away?

Landon Sure. And don't feel bad. It's okay.

(Sister smiles and they go off stage. Brother and Landon return.)

Brother (To Landon) You mean you surprised Dad and cleaned out the garage? When I looked in, I thought I was seeing a mirage!

(They leave stage. Mom and Dad and Landon come out.)

Mom Here's your allowance. You've been a big help these days.

Dad Even when I'm sure you would have rather gone out to play.

(They pat him on the back and the three leave.)

SCENE IV

(Night time again. Landon's bedroom. He sleeps. Angel is standing behind him again.)

Angel On Christmas Eve, think of all the wonderful things you've done, and all the nice things you will continue to do. And when you go to the manger, offer them up to Jesus. Those are the kinds of gifts that he likes best.

(Christmas Eve. Jesus, Mary and Joseph, Angel, and any others from the Nativity, like shepherds, etc. Landon kneels before baby Jesus, bows his head and prays. Children sing Christmas carols. After they sing, everyone stands, facing audience. They bow.)

I Love You Coupons Gift Idea

Make your Mom and Dad a card for Christmas. Cut these coupons out and put them inside the card. Mom and Dad can "redeem" each coupon whenever they want. When they give you a coupon, you give them the "gift" on the coupon. What a wonderful surprise for your parents!

Good for one hug COUPON	I will help clean the house COUPON
I will make my bed COUPON	I will pick up my toys COUPON
I will play with my brother or sister COUPON	Good for one hug COUPON
I will go to bed on time COUPON	I will pick up my clothes COUPON
I will help with the dishes COUPON	I will feed the pets COUPON
I will not complain about my dinner COUPON	I will answer in a nice tone of voice COUPON
Good for one hug COUPON	I will share with someone COUPON
I will put on a happy face COUPON	Good for one hug COUPON

Dear God,

I want to start the New Year with a clean slate.

Forgive me for the wrong things I did this past year.

Help me love you with all my heart.

And help me love my neighbor as myself.

I want to be kind to my family and friends,

my classmates and neighbors,

even when it is hard.

With all my heart,

I love you, Lord.

Amen.

Note to Parents and Teachers

Warm up the month of January with these fun activities. Help your youngsters make calendars for their families. Read aloud the story of St. Elizabeth Seton. Celebrate the feast of Epiphany with the crossword puzzle and hidden picture activities. You can also use the Apostles Word Search any time during the year.

For Peace

Holy Spirit,

hear our prayer.

So many people are suffering

because of war and hatred.

Bring peace to our families,

our communities,

our country, and our whole world.

Fill us with your peace.

Amen.

Children's Calendar of the Saints

JANUARY

1 Mary, Mother of God	2 Saints Basil the Great and Gregory Nazianzen	3	4 St. Elizabeth Ann Seton	5 St. John Neumann	6 Epiphany of the Lord Bl. André Bessette	7 St. Raymond of Peñafort
8	9	10	11	12 St. Marguerite Bourgeoys	13 St. Hilary of Poitiers	14
15 St. Paul the Hermit	16	17 St. Anthony of Egypt	18	19	20 St. Fabian, St. Sebastian	21 St. Agnes
22 St. Vincent of Saragossa	23	24 St. Francis de Sales	25 Conversion of St. Paul, Apostle	26 Saints Timothy and Titus	27 St. Angela Merici	28 St. Thomas Aquinas
29	30	31 St. John Bosco				

Month of January

New Year's Gift Idea

Homemade Calendar

Here is a New Year's gift you can give to your family. You can make your own picture or design. Then they can enjoy looking at it all year long!

Materials: 11" x 17" poster paper, 8 1/2" x 11" white piece of paper, markers, colored pencils, or crayons, 12 copies of the calendar sheet (page 42), stapler, glue (stick glue is neater), a pre-printed calendar to see the correct dates for the new year.

Directions:

1. Draw your cover picture horizontally on the 8 1/2" x 11" paper.

2. On the top section of the large poster paper, glue the picture you've drawn.

3. Write in the months, and dates for each month.

4. Staple the 12 calendar sheets together.

5. Glue the back of your December calendar to the bottom section of the poster paper.

SUNDAY	MONDAY	TUESDAY	WEDNESDAY	THURSDAY	FRIDAY	SATURDAY

St. Elizabeth Seton

A Story to Read Aloud

On August 28, 1774 (two years before the American Revolution!) Elizabeth was born to Catherine and Richard Bayley. Elizabeth was baptized into the Episcopal Church. When she was only two years old, her mother died. Elizabeth was very sad during her childhood. Even though her dad remarried and had other children, she could not get along with her new stepmother. But then, when she was almost twenty years old, she became very happy! She fell in love with and married William Seton. They both loved each other very much.

Through the years, Elizabeth grew close to God and helped the poor and needy. In fact, in 1797, she helped to found The Widow's Society. When her father-in-law died in 1798, she and her husband took care of William's younger brothers and sisters, along with their own children.

After their fifth child was born in 1802, Elizabeth noticed that William's health was getting worse. He had tuberculosis. She suggested they go to Italy where the climate was better for him. They took their oldest daughter, Anna, with them and left the other children with relatives. But a year later, in December of 1803, William died in Italy.

While Elizabeth was in Italy, some Catholic friends invited her to their church. Elizabeth learned about the Mass, and she was drawn to the Catholic faith. She read the lives of the saints and teachings of the Church. When she returned to New York, Elizabeth taught her children prayers and hymns and read Bible stories to them. In 1805 she converted to Catholicism. Since her friends and relatives were Episcopalian, many of them were angry at her for changing her religion.

In 1808, Elizabeth started a Catholic school in Baltimore, Maryland. A year later, she became a religious sister. She also became foundress of a group of religious teaching sisters. Elizabeth became known as "Mother Seton." She and her sisters started many Catholic schools in the United States. After years of trials and blessings, she died in 1821. In 1975, Pope Paul VI declared Elizabeth a saint.

Find the Year

After reading this story about St. Elizabeth Seton, find all the years in the story and circle them. Then find those years in the Number Search below. Example: The year of her birth is circled.

8	0	8	1	7	9	7	2	3
9	6	8	9	5	3	6	0	7
7	2	1	7	7	4	8	8	5
1	8	0	5	0	1	4	1	7

Epiphany Hidden Picture

Today we celebrate the visit that three special kings made to little Jesus. They came from far, far away. How did they know where to find Jesus? To give you a clue, color all the shapes with #1 and #2 yellow. Color all the shapes with #3 and #4 in different shades of dark blue.

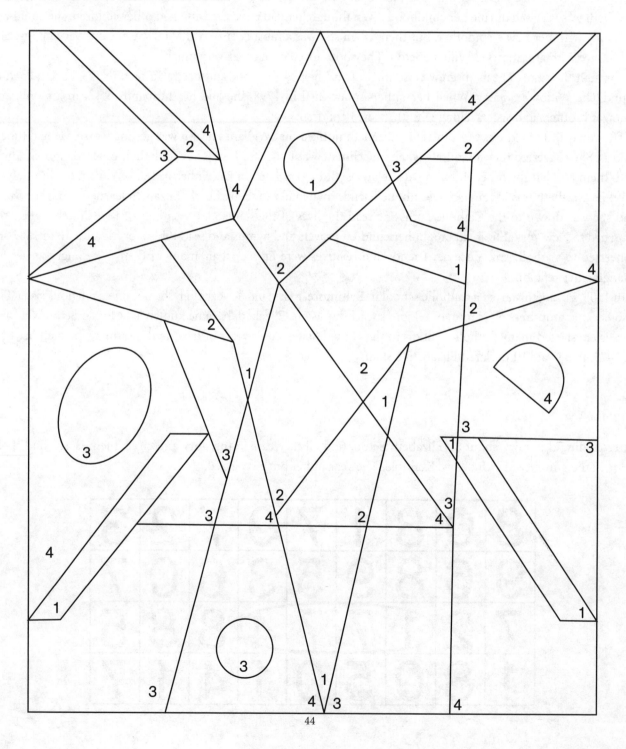

Epiphany Crossword

Test yourself by trying to do this crossword on your own. See how much you know about the story of the three wise men. If you have trouble with any of the answers, read Matthew 2:1–12 with a family member.

Across

1. Another name for the three wise men.

2. The jealous king who reigned at the time of Jesus' birth.

3. Bethlehem is in the land of _____.

4. The Magi came from the _____.

5. They followed the _____.

Down

1. The three kings gave Jesus gifts of gold, frankincense and _____.

3. The three kings paid homage to _____.

6. The wise men were warned in a _____ not to return to Herod.

Apostles Word Search

When Jesus was about 30 years old, he began teaching people the good news of God's kingdom. He chose twelve men to be his close friends. They followed him wherever he went. They are called the Twelve Apostles. To find out more about this, read Matthew 10:1–20.

Here is a word search with all their names.

Peter	Matthew	Andrew	Bartholomew
James	Philip	Thomas	Thaddaeus
John	Simon	James	Judas

```
M W E M O L O H T R A B
S E M A P I L I H P J L
E C K T H A D D A E U S
M F L T S A M O H T D I
A J O H N B Z R Y E A M
J E S E M A J U N R S O
U P R W E R D N A Z Q N
```

Lord Jesus, I want to follow you always!

Month of February

Lord,

winter days are long and cold.

Thank you for our warm home!

Things can seem pretty hard sometimes.

Thank you for the people who encourage us.

Some days we feel lonely or sad.

Thank you for being our friend.

We don't always know the right thing to do.

Thank you for teaching us how to pray.

Our Father,

who art in heaven,

hallowed be thy name

thy kingdom come;

thy will be done

on earth as it is in heaven.

Give us this day our daily bread

and forgive us our trespasses

as we forgive those who trespass against us;

and lead us not into temptation

but deliver us from evil.

Amen.

Note to Parents and Teachers

St. Valentine's Day can be a good introduction to Lent and Easter if we focus on Jesus' love for us and our love for Jesus. Besides the three activities for St. Valentine's Day, you'll find one for the feast of the Presentation and one for Our Lady of Lourdes, which celebrates Mary's appearance to St. Bernadette Soubirous. These last two can also be used during May. Activities for Lent are included in the month of March.

Children's Calendar of the Saints

FEBRUARY

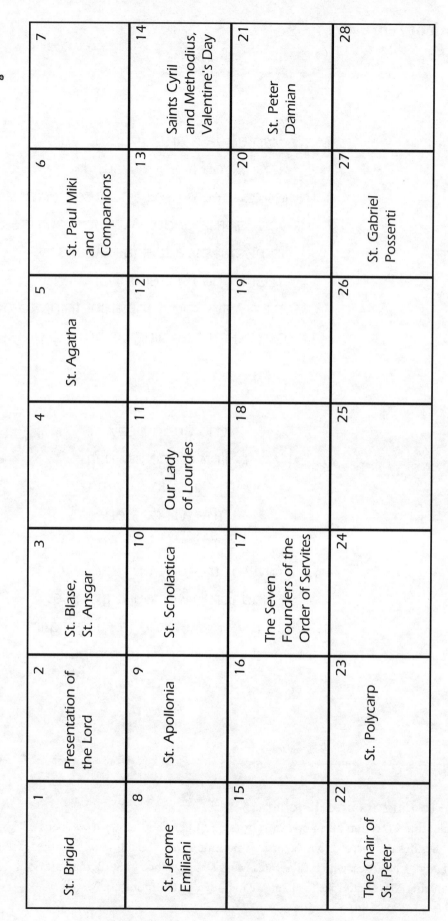

1	2	3	4	5	6	7
St. Brigid	Presentation of the Lord	St. Blase, St. Ansgar		St. Agatha	St. Paul Miki and Companions	
8	9	10	11	12	13	14
St. Jerome Emiliani	St. Apollonia	St. Scholastica	Our Lady of Lourdes			Saints Cyril and Methodius, Valentine's Day
15	16	17	18	19	20	21
		The Seven Founders of the Order of Servites				St. Peter Damian
22	23	24	25	26	27	28
The Chair of St. Peter	St. Polycarp				St. Gabriel Possenti	

Month of February

Feast of the Presentation

Mary and Joseph took baby Jesus to the temple. They offered him to God according to Jewish custom. A holy man named Simeon blessed them. He knew that Jesus was the promised savior.

Help Mary and Joseph find their way to the temple. Connect the dots starting with #1.

.8   .9

.6   .7

.4   .5

.2   .3

.1

49

Our Lady of Lourdes Cryptoquip

February 11th

St. Bernadette was a poor, humble girl who loved Jesus very much. In 1858 the Blessed Virgin appeared to Bernadette near Lourdes, France. During these visions in the cave at Massabielle, Mary called Christians to a change of heart. She asked them to pray more and to help people who were poor and sick. Because of these appearances of Our Lady of Lourdes, many people returned to the faith.

A Message from Our Lady of Lourdes

What was the Blessed Mother's message to St. Bernadette? To find out, use the code to fill in the letters on the blank lines below. The first two words are done for you.

1=O	6=M	11=J	16=X	21=I
2=H	7=F	12=C	17=G	22=K
3=B	8=A	13=S	18=D	23=R
4=L	9=V	14=N	19=P	24=W
5=Q	10=T	15=E	20=I	25=U
				26=Z

I   A   M
20   8   6   10   2   15

20   6   6   8   12   25   4   8   10   15

12   1   14   12   15   19   10   20   1   14

50

Valentine Maze

Help me find my way to Jesus!

Valentine Puzzle

In one of his letters to the Corinthians, St. Paul tells us how to practice love (1 Cor 13).

Materials: Glue, scissors, poster paper, crayons

Instructions: Color and cut out the entire heart and glue it to poster paper. Then cut out the shapes to make your own puzzle.

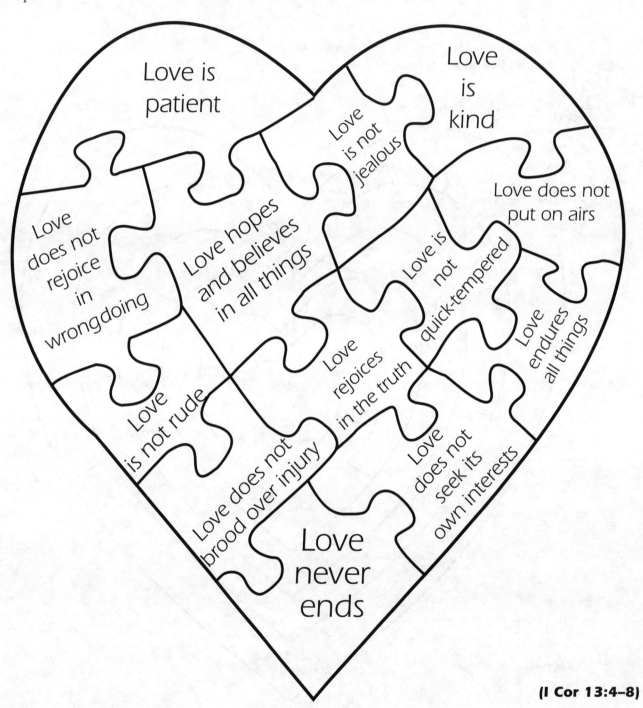

(I Cor 13:4–8)

Month of February

Love Crossword

Ask a family member to read 1 Corinthians, chapter 13 with you. Then finish the sentences below. Use the words you filled in to complete the crossword. (Depending on the version of the Bible you use, the words may be a little different from the ones in your Bible.)

How many ways can you say "I love you" to your family, friends, and neighbors?

Across

2. Love is _____.

3. Love does not put on _____.

5. Love _____ all things.

7. Love_____ with the truth.

9. Love is not _____.

11. Love never _____.

12. Love does not brood over _____.

Down

1. Love is not _____.

4. Love is not _____.

6. Love _____ all things.

8. Love does not seek its own _____.

10. Love is _____.

For the times we hurt others with our words or actions,

we are sorry, Lord.

For the times when we had a chance to do something good

but didn't do it,

we are sorry, Lord.

For our angry or jealous thoughts,

we are sorry, Lord.

For the times when we didn't obey or respect

our parents and teachers,

we are sorry, Lord.

Jesus,

you are so full of love and compassion;

even when you suffered, you forgave those who hurt you.

Help us become good disciples.

Jesus, make our hearts as loving as yours.

Amen.

Note to Parents and Teachers

March offers us so many "teachable moments": the feastdays of two popular saints; the feast of the Annunciation to Mary; and, of course, the holy season of Lent. As you share the saints activities with your children, talk about what you can learn from them. Use the lenten activities to focus on the season's message of reconciliation and renewal. You will find Easter activities in the month of April.

Children's Calendar of the Saints

MARCH

1 St. David	**2**	**3** St. Katharine Drexel	**4** St. Casimir	**5**	**6**	**7** Saints Perpetua and Felicity
8 St. John of God	**9** St. Frances of Rome	**10**	**11**	**12**	**13**	**14**
15	**16**	**17** St. Patrick	**18** St. Cyril of Jerusalem	**19** St. Joseph, Husband of Mary	**20**	**21**
22	**23** St. Turibius de Mongrovejo	**24**	**25** Annunciation of the Lord	**26**	**27**	**28**
29	**30**	**31**				

St. Patrick's Day Pictogram

St. Patrick was born in 385 A.D. When he was young, he was sold into slavery. His master made him take care of the sheep. Patrick later became a priest and then a bishop in Ireland. He loved Jesus very much and taught many people about the Catholic faith. We honor him for his bravery and his dedication.

Decode the message about St. Patrick. The pictogram will give you clues. Fill in the letters on the blank lines below. Then combine and unscramble the boxed letters to complete the message. The first one is done for you.

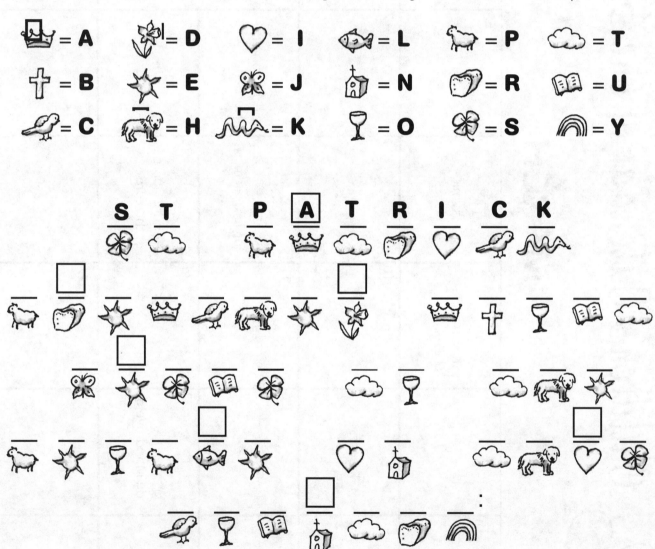

Feast of St. Joseph

St. Joseph was a holy man. God chose him to be the husband of Mary and the foster father of Jesus. God asked him to do some difficult things. But Joseph had faith and courage. He said "yes" and obeyed God. St. Joseph was poor and worked hard as a carpenter his whole life. But he never quit what he started. He took good care of Jesus and Mary. He was their provider and protector. Now from heaven he watches over our families.

Word Search
Look for the following words. They may be up, down, backward, or across.

baby	dove	lily	patron
bread	foster father	man	protector
carpenter	holy	Mary	ring
chosen by God	husband	mission	saint
Church	Joseph	obedient	tools

```
M A N R O T C E T O R P
M C H O S E N B Y G O D
I H U B L R K L P E C Y
S C S E T E Y I A V F L
S R B D N T B L T O E O
I U A I I N A Y R D B H
O H N E A E B T O O L S
N C D N S P O M N S E P
F O S T E R F A T H E R
G N I R Q A M D A E R B
H Y R A M C J O S E P H
```

St. Joseph's Crown

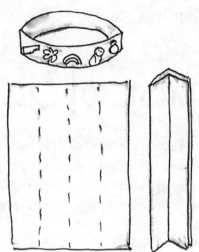

Materials: markers, glitter glue, glue, tape

Instructions: Take a piece of paper measuring 8 1/2" x 11". Fold the paper lengthwise once, then again so that you have four even columns. Cut along folds to make four long strips, two for each crown. Copy, color, and cut out the symbols of St. Joseph below. Paste them on the front strip of paper. Use glitter glue and markers or crayons to decorate the rest of the paper. After it is dry, tape it to the back strip so that the crown is the right size to fit your head.

St. Joseph Poster

During the month of March, honor St. Joseph by making a poster for your home or religion class. If you want, copy and color the picture below. Then say these short prayers to St. Joseph:

St. Joseph, pray for us.

St. Joseph, provide for us.

The Annunciation of the Lord

Connect the dots to see who is visiting Mary. Then read Luke 1:26–38.

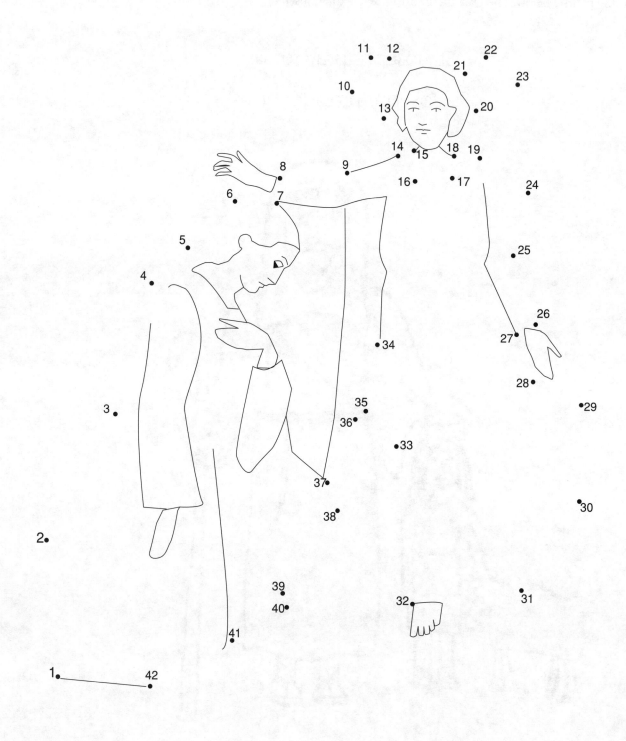

Special Secrets Decoding Game

When you have a secret, you share it with someone you trust, like a parent or your best friend. You tell them, "This is just between you and me," which makes it even more special. During the season of Lent, the Church encourages us to take extra time to pray, to fast, and to do kind things for others.

First, solve the list of clues below and write the answers on the blank lines with the numbers under them. The first clue and answer have been done for you. Then decode Jesus' special message to you by matching each letter to its correct number. After you have finished, ask an adult to read Matthew 6:1–18 with you.

You fry french fries in hot...

O I L
2 40 19

Jack and Jill went up this

8 25 20 41

Hello!

22 31

An artist can do this

48 4 6 39

Opposite of "over"

51 29 27 9 43

Squirrels eat these

32 3 24 14

A long way

5 46 36

Hens do this with eggs

42 18 1

Opposite of "No"

49 16 33

Farm animal with udders

35 28 11

A pair

38 45 13

Wipe off a chalkboard

15 10 23 26 37

A flower symbolizing "Love"

47 50 17 34

You chew with them

7 30 44 21 12

1 Y	2 O	3 U	4 R	5	6	7	8	9	10	11	12	13	
14	15	16	17	18	19	20	21	22	23	24		25	26
27	28	29	30	31	32	33	34	35	36	37	38		
39	40	41	42	43	44	45	46	47	48		49	50	51

Lenten Silhouette

Jesus carried his cross without complaining because of his great love for each of us. Sometimes we may not feel like doing something—cleaning our room, helping our parents, being kind to our sister or brother. But when we do something for love of Jesus, we help him carry his cross. Make a special sign to help you remember to help Jesus carry his cross during Lent.

Materials: Colored chalk, white copier paper, hairspray, black construction paper, black marker
Instructions: Take a piece of copier paper and rub chalk on it with a rainbow of colors. Spray it with hairspray to keep the chalk dust from getting all over. Let it dry a few minutes. Next, draw and cut a cross and a "hill" out of the black construction paper. Make a sign like the one below, using the cross as your letter "t," and finishing the sentence (with black marker), "take up your cross." Hang it where you can see it often.

Black construction paper   Colorful chalk background

ake up your cross

Matthew 16:24

Grow Like a Flower

Have you ever seen a flower garden? There are so many colors. When you look at them, you say, "Oh, how pretty they are!" But each flower can't be beautiful unless it has sprouted and grown to be the kind of flower God wanted it to be. God has a plan for us, too. Our bodies grow when we eat and exercise right. Our minds "grow" when we study hard in school. Our hearts become bigger and more full of love when we show love, pray, and do what is right. Now, you can make a special poster to help everyone see how you are growing in love for Jesus. You can start by putting a seed at the bottom of the paper. By Easter time you will have a beautiful flower!

Materials :
• Poster paper
• Construction paper
  8 1" pieces of green paper for the stem
  4 leaves cut from construction paper
  1 cut-out circle for the middle of the flower
  A number of different/same colored petals
• White yarn for roots, 3-5 pieces
• Markers, glitter, glue

Directions: On the bottom of the poster paper, cut a half-piece of brown construction paper for the "dirt." Draw or cut a "seed" out of colored paper. Paste that down in the "dirt." Every time you pray or give up something for Jesus or do something nice for someone, you can add, in the order listed above, one of the following things (remember, glue only one thing down for each good thing you do.) You can add with markers or glitter glue anything else you want, like a sky, or sun, or butterfly, etc. Then, write at the top of the poster, "God's Beautiful Flower." Be sure to put your own name on it somewhere so everyone can see how you have grown.

Imagine...

This special activity will be like a "thinking prayer." Some people call it a form of "meditation." You will need quiet time. Turn off the radio and the television. With a family member, read one of these Scripture passages: Luke 23:26–56; John 18:1—19:42. Using the list of characters below, choose who—you would like to have been. Close your eyes and think about what it would be like to be that person. What did you see? What did you feel? Think of details in the scene, like a look that Jesus gave to you, or someone crying beside you. What did you say to Jesus?

Pilate

Simon of Cyrene

One of the holy women of Jerusalem

The good thief

The centurion

One of Jesus' friends

Joseph of Arimathea

Woman who anointed Jesus' body after he died

Mary, Jesus' mother

Mary's sister (wife of Clopas)

Mary Magdalene

John "Disciple whom he loved"

Nicodemus

In the Garden

What was Jesus' prayer?
(Lk 22:42–43)

Near the end of his life, Jesus knew that he was going to suffer very much. Though he was afraid of what was to come, Jesus loved his Father. He wanted to do his Father's will.

Below, find out what Jesus prayed. Take a black marker. Cross out the first letter of the phrase and every other letter after that. What do the letters spell? Copy these words on a blank sheet of paper. Color and decorate it. Be creative!

GFKAMTIHZESR,

FLBECTA YGONUERH

WJIBLULP BMEO DKOLNCE,

FNUOZTS MRILNCEH

Jesus,

Every hour, every day

with all creation I say:

"Jesus my Redeemer lives!"

You died and rose, there is no doubt;

I know what life is all about.

I'm so glad my Redeemer lives!

You are alive and you are risen.

I'll show my love in each decision,

because Jesus my Redeemer lives!

Heavenly Father, Spirit, and Son,

be with me 'till my days are done,

and I will pray forever, "My Redeemer lives!"

Note to Parents and Teachers

Easter, spring, new life! Enjoy making the jelly bean nest with your youngsters. Use the word search and/or Thomas Believes as a starting point to talk about how important the resurrection is to our Christian faith. The Noah's Ark and Spring Picture Find activities can help your youngsters be more aware of the wonders of spring.

Children's Calendar of the Saints

APRIL

1	2	3	4	5	6	7
	St. Francis of Paola		St. Isidore of Seville	St. Vincent Ferrer		St. John Baptiste de la Salle
8	9	10	11	12	13	14
			St. Stanislaus		St. Martin I	
15	16	17	18	19	20	21
						St. Anselm
22	23	24	25	26	27	28
	St. George, St. Adelbert	St. Fidelis	St. Mark the Evangelist			St. Peter Chanel, St. Louis Mary de Montfort
29	30					
St. Catherine of Siena	St. Pius V					

Easter Word Search

Find the following words. Then use them to tell the story of Easter.

Alleluia	Glorious	Life	Praise
Angels	God	Lord	Resurrection
Easter	Jesus	Love	Risen
Empty tomb	King	Peace	

```
N A I U L E L L A B P Z
E M P T Y T O M B K R Y
A L E G R L R S I I A S
S S A P O N D N S N I L
T U C V U D G E L G S E
E S E F I L N J V O E G
R E S U R R E C T I O N
M J S U O I R O L G K A
```

Thomas Believes

(Jn 20:28)

At first, Thomas did not believe that Jesus rose from the dead. He said, "I won't believe it until I see it." A week later, even though the doors of the hiding place were locked, Jesus appeared to his friends. Thomas was with them. Imagine the surprise Thomas had! He could not doubt the risen Christ this time. What did he exclaim when he saw Jesus standing there?

To find out, look at the clock below. Start at the letter "M." On the lines below, write down every other letter, going clockwise.

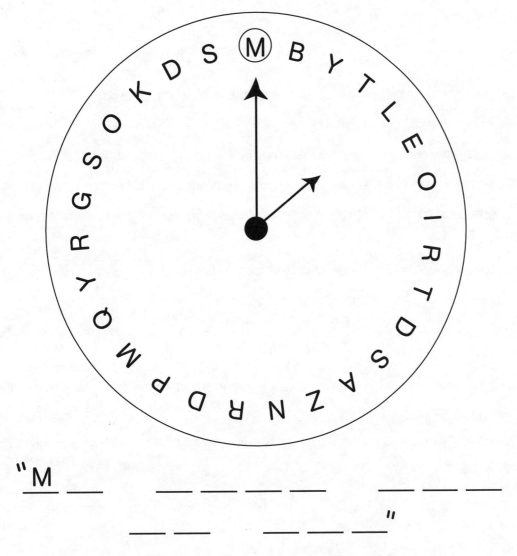

"M __   __ __ __ __   __ __

__ __ __   __ __ __"

Jesus tells us what he told Thomas:
Blessed are they who have not seen me but still believe!

Easter

Easter News

Write a short news article about Jesus' resurrection. You can write it as an interview with eyewitnesses, using the questions below to help you. Look in the Bible for help with your information:

Matthew 28:1–20

Mark 16:1–20

Luke 24:1–53

John 20:1—21:25

1. According to your source, Matthew, what frightened the guards at the tomb?

2. Excuse me, ladies, what did you see at the tomb, and what was your reaction?

3. According to an eyewitness, what did Jesus tell the disciples on the mountain?

4. According to another source, Mark, why did the risen Jesus reproach the eleven disciples?

5. Before his death, Jesus had chosen twelve apostles. On that first Easter, why were there only eleven apostles?

6. Your source, Luke, can tell about the event on the road to Emmaus. Just recap the highlights.

7. John, who raced with you to the tomb? What did you find?

8. Mary Magdalene, who did you think Jesus was at first? What did you say to him? What did he say to you?

9. That evening, even with the doors locked, Jesus came and stood among the gathered disciples. John, what did he say to you all?

10. Thomas, what finally made you believe that Jesus truly rose from the dead? What did Jesus tell you? How did you respond?

Month of April

Jelly Bean Nest

Easter Activity

Here is something special you and your family can make for Easter!

Ingredients: 1 cup of sugar, 1 cup of white corn syrup, 1 1/2 cups of peanut butter, 1 tsp. of vanilla, 6 cups of regular sized Chinese noodles, 1 bag of multi-colored jelly beans, 1/2 bag of coconut, green food coloring

Directions: Ask an adult to help you. First, boil the sugar and corn syrup together. Remove from the heat. Add the peanut butter and vanilla (be careful not to burn yourself). Stir it until it is mixed well. Pour it over the Chinese noodles and mix everything together. Put it in a big bowl or round cake pan and as it hardens, shape it into a "nest." Let cool. Put the coconut in a zip-lock bag and add a drop or two of food coloring. Knead the bag and watch the coconut turn green. This will be the "grass" you put inside the nest. Next, add the jelly beans. As your final touch, cut out or copy this poem to place in the center of the nest. Now you have a wonderful centerpiece for Easter!

P.S. If you want to make tiny nests to pass out, just mold the mixture into muffin pans instead of in the big bowl.

Here is a treat for my Easter guest:

See the jelly beans in this nest

Yellow, orange, pink, and green,

These are the colors of the spring.

Then look at the bean that is red,

That one is for the blood he shed

Purple and black mean sorrow for sin,

But white is the grace we receive from him

To God all praise and glory be:

Our risen Lord has set us free!

Happy Easter!

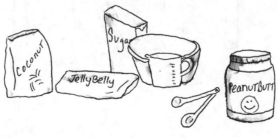

Noah's Ark

My own booklet to read and color

During the spring and the "April Showers," it is fun to remember the story of Noah. Here is a booklet to read and color. Fold each page in half so that pages follow in order. Then staple the sheets together at the fold.

NOAH'S ARK

My own booklet to read and color

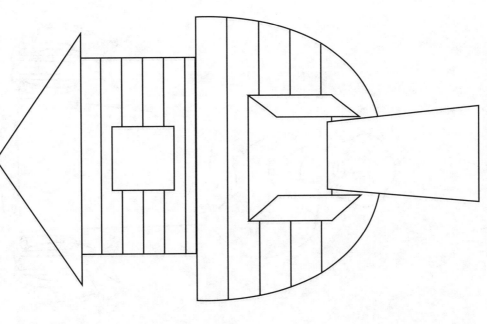

Noah built the ark;
that's what God said to do.

1.

that God would never send
such rain to flood the earth again.

8.

God told Noah the rainbow
was a sign of his promise, then,
7.

Then he gathered up the animals
and put them in two by two.
2.

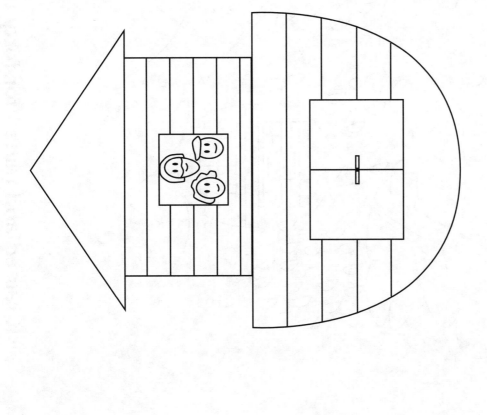

Once the doors of the ark were locked and God's people were safe and sound.

3.

Then the sun came out and Noah saw a rainbow in the sky!

6.

It rained and rained for forty days;
nothing on earth was dry.
5.

the thunder rolled, the clouds burst open;
the rain came pouring down.
4.

Month of April

It's Spring! Picture Find

Spring is fun! We can look around outside and see the leaves bud. We can see the baby birds in their nests, and the grass starting to turn green. We praise God for all creation!

Can you find the pictures below?

Month of May

Blessed Mary,

you were chosen to be

the mother of the Son of God.

What an honor that was!

Even the angel Gabriel knew it

when he said,

"Blessed are you among women..."

Mary, watch over each of us.

Teach us how to love God

as you did.

Help keep us close

to your son, Jesus.

Hail Mary, full of grace.

The Lord is with you.

Blessed are you among women

and blessed is the fruit of your womb, Jesus.

Holy Mary, mother of God,

pray for us sinners now

and at the hour of our death.

Amen.

Note to Parents and Teachers

Activities for the month of May include: a maze and a matching game for Good Shepherd Sunday (which is also the Day of Prayer for Vocations); two gift-making projects for Mother's Day; a Hand Fan craft project for hot summer days; and a pictogram that can be used any time.

Children's Calendar of the Saints

May

1 St. Joseph, the Worker	**2** St. Athanasius	**3** Saints Philip and James, Apostles	**4**	**5**	**6**	**7**
8	**9**	**10** Blessed Damien de Veuster of Molokai	**11**	**12** Saints Nereus and Achilleus, St. Pancras	**13**	**14** St. Matthias, Apostle
15 St. Isidore the Farmer	**16**	**17**	**18** St. John I	**19**	**20** St. Bernardine of Siena	**21**
22	**23**	**24**	**25** St. Bede, St. Gregory VII, St. Mary Magdalen de Pazzi	**26** St. Philip Neri	**27** St. Augustine of Canterbury	**28**
29	**30** St. Joan of Arc	**31** Visitation of the Blessed Virgin Mary				

Month of May

The Good Shepherd Maze

Jesus told his friends a story. It was about a shepherd who had 100 sheep. One got lost. The shepherd was very worried about it. So he left all the rest of the sheep in order to find that one lost lamb.

   Now pretend that you are there, too. The shepherd asks you to help him search for his little animal. Where do you suppose it is? In the maze below, begin at "start." Make a path with your pencil or crayon. You can go up or down or sideways in any direction, but not diagonally. Without skipping any letters, see if you can find the lamb! The words below tell where the lamb is. Follow the letters that spell out these words:

OVER THE HILL DOWN THE SANDY PATH AROUND THE THREE BIG TREES EATING GRASS BY THE CREEK

Start

O	V	E	R	T	L	U	N	D	T	B
A	P	G	N	H	M	O	E	E	H	E
O	D	L	S	E	Y	R	B	R	H	T
W	F	L	I	H	K	A	I	R	E	E
N	K	Y	P	A	T	H	G	T	F	S
T	M	D	S	A	R	G	G	N	R	E
H	B	N	S	T	H	R	G	I	T	A
E	S	A	B	Y	E	C	R	E	E	K

End

What Do I Want to Be?

Here are some words you may have heard before, but you may not know their exact meaning. Match up each word with its correct definition by writing the definition's letter next to the word. If you are not sure, ask a parent or teacher for help. The first one is done for you.

Vocation __E__

Witness _____

Religious Sister _____

Priest _____

Religious Brother _____

Missionary _____

Saint _____

Ministry _____

A. One who tells other people about what he knows or what he has seen. As a Christian, this person is a "light for all to see."

B. A specific work a person or group of people do in order to serve the Church.

C. An ordained minister who receives power to say Mass and administer the sacraments. He devotes his entire life to God and God's people.

D. A woman who takes the vows of poverty, chastity, and obedience and lives in a community with other women who choose to do the same.

E. A way of life to which a person feels God has called him or her.

F. A man who takes the vows of poverty, chastity, and obedience and lives in a community with other men who choose to do the same.

G. A lay person, religious, or priest who leaves their own country to go to another to preach the gospel and inspire others to follow Christ.

H. A holy person who strives to love God and neighbor. Every Christian is called to be one. Those who are canonized are believed to be in heaven and can intercede on our behalf.

Mother's Day Gift Idea
A Chair for Mom

Here is a project you can work on for your Mom for Mother's Day. It is a card and a gift all in one. And it is very easy to make.

Materials:
Copy of chair on the following page, small pieces of material for chair "cushion," construction paper, plastic "eye" (optional), crayons or markers, safety scissors, glue

Here's a chair for you to sit in,
Put your feet up, do some knittin'.
Then I'll try to do my best
So you can finally take a rest.
I'll clear the dishes, use the broom,
Pick up my toys and clean the room.
I'll do all this without a fit
And then with you I'll come and sit.
I hope you'll hold me a little while–
Tell me a story, share a smile.
I love you, Mom, and I want to say
I hope this chair has made your day!

Directions: Ask an adult to help you with the cutting. First, color and cut out the picture of the chair on the next page. Paste it onto your favorite color of construction paper. Glue a plastic eye on or color in the eye that is there. If you would like to add more things, you could even put hair and a hat on it. Then, cut out the poem along the rounded lines on the next page. Fold in half and glue the back of the bottom half to the seat of the chair. Cut out and glue a piece of material to the back of the top half of the poem. When dry, fold the top half over the bottom half, which will make it look like a cushion on your chair. You may write the words, "A Chair for You, Mom" at the top of the poem, and sign at the bottom, "With Love from…" Be sure to pick a day to do what the poem says in order to make this a wonderful gift for your Mom.

Poem
Here

Fold here in half

Heart Flowers

Mother's Day Gift Idea

Here is something that will make your mom smile on Mother's Day. She can put it anywhere and the "flowers" will last all year long!

Materials:

Empty tuna can, cleaned and spray-painted on the outside; play dough; popsicle sticks; construction paper; hole puncher; yarn; tape; markers; glue; glitter glue (optional); tempera paint

Directions:

1. Cut out the heart on the next page. Take three of your favorite colors of construction paper and trace the heart two times on each paper. Cut out the three sets of hearts.
2. As in figure "A," take the first set and glue about 1/4 of one end of a popsiciile stick onto the bottom of the heart. Then glue the other heart directly on top of the first heart, making the stick the "stem" of the flower. Let it dry.
3. Punch holes along the upper edges of the heart. Take a 12" piece of yarn and put a small piece of scotch tape around the end of the yarn to make it easy to push through the holes in the heart. Like a sewing card, take the heart and "sew" it with the yarn, all the way around. Knot the ends near the "stem."
4. Color, cut, and paste the spool on the heart. With markers write "I Love You SEW much!" You may wish to highlight "SEW" with glitter glue.
5. Now, look at figure "B." Glue the popsicle stick in between the second set of hearts as you did before. Decorate a happy face on one side. On the back write, "You Make My Heart Happy!"
6. Fold the last set of hearts in half (Figure "C"). Then cut two horizontal slits. Unfold the heart and cut one vertical slit on the right. This makes a "door" in the heart. Glue the hearts together, only along the edges, with the stick as the stem as you did before. After it is dried, open the "door" and write "Mom."
7. On the outside of the heart, or on the backside, write, "You are Always IN my heart." You may decorate each heart any way you want.
8. Finally, trace and cut out the "leaves" to glue onto the stem. After everything has dried, put play dough inside the (pre-spray-painted) tuna can. Across the front of the can you can paint the word "MOM." Stick the flower "stems" inside the play dough. Now you have a bouquet you can give to your mom.

I ♥ you 🧵 sew much!

Figure A

MOM

Front   Figure C

You are always in my heart

Back

cut   cut   Front   Figure B

You make my heart happy!

Back

85

Hand Fan
Summer Activity

Get ready for a hot summer! Make a fan for yourself or make a bunch with your friends.

Materials:
Thick white poster paper
Tongue depressor or popsicle stick
Markers
Scissors and craft glue

Directions:
1. Trace the shape of the fan—found on the next page—onto white poster paper.
2. Choose your favorite quote from the Bible or a special phrase you like. Use markers to write it on the fan.
3. Add colorful drawings like a cross, or a sun, or a rainbow, etc. You can decorate both sides of the fan!
4. When you are done with that, glue the tongue depressor onto the bottom back side.

Here are some phrases you might like to use for your project:
    Smile, God loves you!
    Praise the Lord for he is good!
    Lord, I place my trust in you!
    My Lord and my God!
    You are my salvation, Lord!

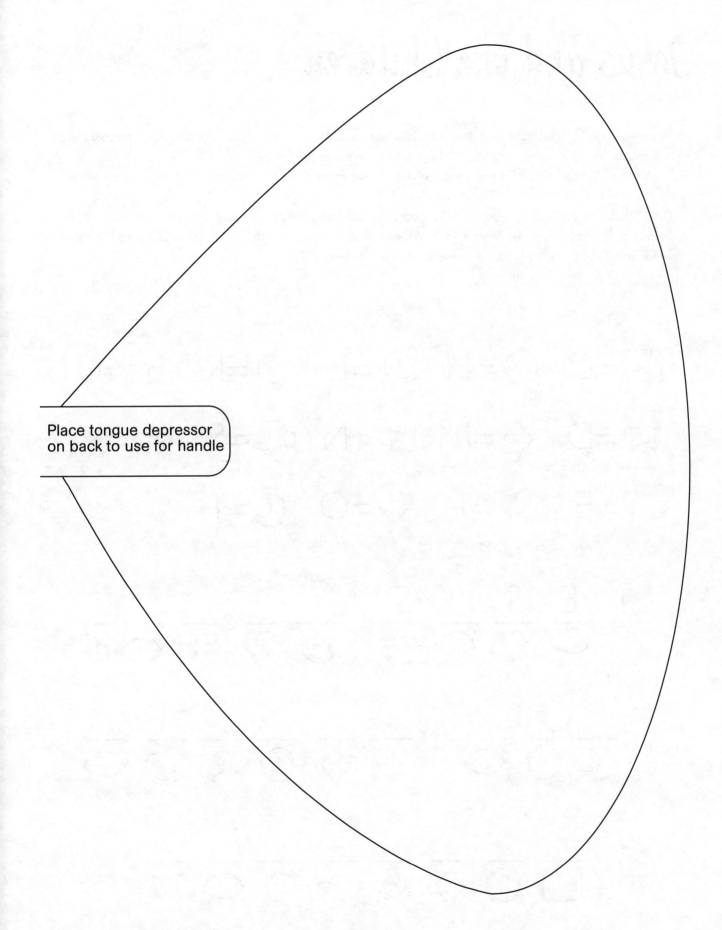

Place tongue depressor
on back to use for handle

Jesus and the Children

(Mt 19:13 / Mk 10:13)

One day, some parents brought their sons and daughters to visit Jesus. But the disciples worried that all the children were bothering Jesus. So they told the boys and girls, "Go away!"

But Jesus was glad the children were there. He said, "Don't make them go. Leave them alone! Heaven belongs to such as these." Jesus hugged the children and blessed them.

   If you want, you can imagine yourself sitting on Jesus' lap and giving him a hug. He loves you so much! In the code, each shape has a matching letter. Use the code to fill in the letters on the line at the bottom. The first word is done for you. Find out what Jesus wants you to remember always.

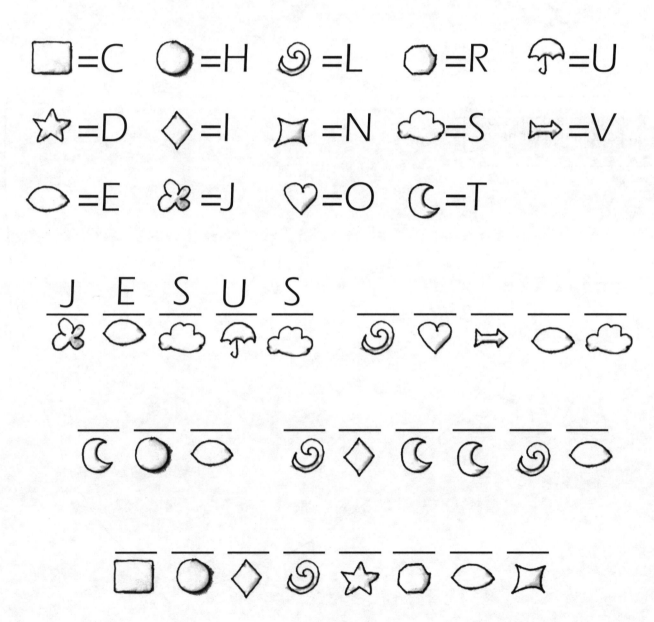

88

End of the School Year

Loving God,
we offer you this past school year
and all the things we have learned.

Please bless our teachers for
their patience and goodness.

This summer
help us remember that we need to
take time out to pray,
even on vacation.

Help us, Lord,
to grow day by day
in wisdom, age and grace,
as Jesus did.
Amen.

Children's Calendar of the Saints

June

1	2	3	4	5	6	7
St. Justin	Saints Marcellinus and Peter	St. Charles Lwanga and Companions		St. Boniface	St. Norbert	
8	9	10	11	12	13	14
	St. Ephrem		St. Barnabas, Apostle		St. Anthony of Padua	
15	16	17	18	19	20	21
				St. Romuald		St. Aloysius Gonzaga
22	23	24	25	26	27	28
St. Paulinus of Nola, St. John Fisher, St. Thomas More		Nativity of St. John the Baptist			St. Cyril of Alexandria	St. Irenaeus
29	30					
Saints Peter and Paul, Apostles	First Martyrs of the Church in Rome					

Children's Calendar of the Saints

July

1	2	3	4	5	6	7
Blessed Junipero Serra		St. Thomas, Apostle	St. Elizabeth of Portugal, Independence Day	St. Anthony Mary Zaccaria		
8	9	10	11	12	13	14
			St. Benedict		St. Henry	
15	16	17	18	19	20	21
St. Bonaventure	Our Lady of Mount Carmel		St. Camillus de Lellis			St. Lawrence of Brindisi
22	23	24	25	26	27	28
St. Mary Magdalene	St. Bridget of Sweden		St. James, Apostle	Saints Joachim and Anne		
29	30	31				
St. Martha	St. Peter Chrysologus	St. Ignatius of Loyola				

Blessed Kateri Tekakwitha (14)

Children's Calendar of the Saints

August

1	2	3	4	5	6	7
St. Alphonsus Ligouri	St. Eusebius of Vercelli, St. Peter Julian Eymard		St. John Vianney	Dedication of the Basilica of St. Mary in Rome	Transfiguration of the Lord	St. Sixtus II and Companions, St. Cajetan
8	9	10	11	12	13	14
St. Dominic		St. Lawrence	St. Clare of Assisi		Saints Pontian and Hippolytus	St. Maximilian Mary Kolbe
15	16	17	18	19	20	21
Assumption of the Blessed Virgin Mary	St. Stephen of Hungary		St. Jane Frances de Chantel	St. John Eudes	St. Bernard	St. Pius X
22	23	24	25	26	27	28
Queenship of the Blessed Virgin Mary	St. Rose of Lima	St. Bartholomew	St. Louis, St. Joseph Calasanz		St. Monica	St. Augustine
29	30	31				
Martyrdom of St. John the Baptist						

Answers to the Puzzles

Page 11 "Treat others as you would like them to treat you."

Page 12

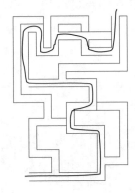

Page 13 Ruler, lunch, paper, crayon, book
"Play fair, Pray to God, Study, Behave, Respect teachers, Listen"

Page 16 "See I am sending an angel before you to guard you on the way and bring you to the place I have prepared."

Page 18 and 19
Across: 1. Church 2. Pray 7. Sacraments 10. Respect
12. Love 13. Truth 15.Thankful 16. Trust 17. Bible
18. Forgive
Down: 1. Christ 3. Peace 4. Honor 5. Happy 6. Defend
8. Courage 9. Sorry 11. Honest 14. Heaven

Page 20 "I will follow Jesus"

Page 21 A. Six B. Three C. Four D. Twelve E. Five, Two
F. One G. Seven H. Ten I. Eleven J. Eight K. Nine

Page 25 "Save us Lord!" "Why are you frightened?"

Page 26 Circle: boat #2, fish #3, Jesus (man #1), clouds #2, sun #1, men #3

Page 27 Dot-to-dot makes a crown

Page 28 1. Christmas 2. Purple 3. Wreath 4. Weeks
5. Pray 6. Four 7. Jesus 8. Pink 9. Friends 10. Reason

Page 29

Page 32 Connect: Mary and Joseph with Baby Jesus; Christmas tree with decorations and lights; Shepherds with sheep; Kings with star

Page 33

Page 34 "Oh come let us adore Him!"

Page 43

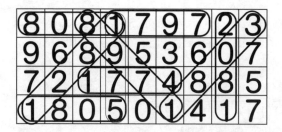

Page 44 Hidden Picture: a star

Page 45

Across: 1.Magi 2.Herod 3.Judah 4.East 5.Star
Down: 1.Myrrh 3.Jesus 6.Dream

Page 46

Page 49 Dots connect stairs to the temple

Page 50 "I am the Immaculate Conception"

Page 51

Page 53

Across: 2.Patient 3.Airs 5.Hopes 7.Rejoices 9.Quick-tempered 11.Ends 12.Injury
Down: 1.Jealous 4.Rude 6.Endures 8.Interests 10.Kind

Page 56 St. Patrick preached about Jesus to the people in this country: Ireland.

Page 57

Page 60 Annunciation Dot-to-Dot: Angel and Mary
  God sent the angel Gabriel to visit Mary. The angel told her that God was pleased with her. He said, "Don't be afraid because you have won God's favor. You will conceive and have a son. You will name him Jesus." Mary said, "How can this be since I do not know man?" The angel assured her, "The power of the Most High will overshadow you... This child will be holy and will be called Son of God." The angel then told her about her cousin Elizabeth who was pregnant, even though she was very old. He said, "Nothing is impossible with God." Mary said, "I am God's servant. Let it happen to me as you have said." Then the angel left her.

Page 61 Clues in order: oil, hill, hi, draw, under, nuts, far, lay, yes, cow, two, erase, rose, teeth.
Message: Your Father who sees all that is done in secret will reward you.

Page 65 Father, let your will be done, not mine

Page 68

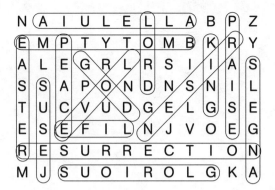

Page 69 "My Lord and My God!"

Page 80

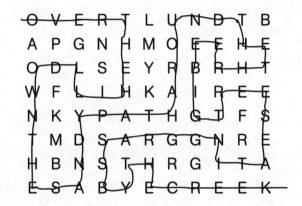

Page 81

Vocation= "E"

Witness= "A"

Religious Sister= "D"

Priest= "C"

Religious Brother= "F"

Missionary= "G"

Saint= "H"

Ministry= "B"

Page 88 "Jesus loves the little children"

Of Related Interest

**100 Creative Teaching Techniques
for Religion Teachers**
Phyllis vos Wezeman

A wealth of practical possibilities for telling and
reviewing the stories of Scripture and faith to
their classes.
1-58595-141-2, 112 pp, $12.95 (J-89)

100 Fun Ways to Livlier Lessons
Maxine Inkel, SL

Refreshing, self-contained activities for children
(grades 2-5) that offer catechists a wealth of
quick, creative, and flexible ways to observe holy
days and holidays throughout the school year.
0-89622-654-9, 128 pp, $14.95 (M-41)

Echo Stories for Children
Celebrating Saints and Seasons in Word and Action
Page McKean Zyromski

These 20 delightful stories involve children in the
"telling" voice and body and students imitate and
mirror the teacher's voice and actions.
0-89622-930-0, 168 pp, $19.95 (B-76)

Jesus & Mary in the Rosary
*Echo Stories for Children
Learners Mimic the Words
and Actions of the Storyteller*
Page McKean Zyromski

Helps catechists teach children the main events in
the lives of Jesus and Mary as described in the
mysteries of the Rosary.
1-58595-140-4, 144 pp, $19.95 (J-87)

School Year Activities for Religion Classes
Gwen Costello

These creative "hands-on" activities are for every
month of the school year and take just five to ten
minutes. They can all be used to supplement
almost any lesson in any textbook series.
1-58595-107-2, 64 pp, $7.95 (J-68)

Available at religious bookstores or from:

TWENTY-THIRD PUBLICATIONS
A Division of Bayard PO BOX 180 • MYSTIC, CT 06355
1-800-321-0411 • FAX: 1-800-572-0788 • E-MAIL: ttpubs@aol.com
www.twentythirdpublications.com
Call for a free catalog